Diaries of an Autistic Superfan

How following The Wiggles all over the world for two decades changed my life.

By

Yahya Lutfi

Diaries of an Autistic Superfan

Me Youniversity Publishing

ISBN-13: 978-1-956565-13-3

Nothing in this book or any affiliations with this book is a substitute for medical or psychological help. If you need assistance, please seek it.

Cover design by Tara Ijai

Photo Credits: Sue Lutfi

Diaries of an Autistic Superfan

Dedication

To my parents who have always supported me and let me try with everything I wanted to.

I also want to thank all of my friends and therapists who have also supported me in everything I have tried to do.

Yahya Lutfi

#OwnVoices

Diaries of an Autistic Superfan

Table of Contents

Note from the Publisher

Autistic people face a wide range of reactions from others, ranging from complete acceptance to uncaring ignorance.

Unfortunately, even those who care for autistic family members, coworkers, and friends may not fully comprehend autism. This results in stereotypes, which can lead to hatred, embarrassment, or other unpleasant situations. You can help others in your community cope with autism by learning more about it.

Many people believe that being autistic is synonymous with being a genius in some way. While it is true that some autistic people have exceptional math, music, and art skills, this is far from the majority—in fact, only a small percentage of autistic people function outside of the normal range in any skill. This stereotype is perpetuated in films and on television because the story of a gifted person overcoming obstacles (such as autism) makes for a compelling plot. However, this is not the norm, and an autistic person should be expected to do no more than their best.

Autism, also known as autism spectrum disorder (ASD), is a broad range of conditions characterized by difficulties with social skills, repetitive behaviors, speech, and nonverbal communication. Autism affects approximately one in every 44 children in the United States today, according to the Centers for Disease Control.

Autism symptoms usually appear by the age of two or three. Some developmental delays can appear even earlier, and it is often diagnosed as early as 18 months.

However, it's critical to recognize that autism is not a form of intellectual development disorder. Although some autistic people have delayed cognitive development, the vast majority do not and should not be treated as such.

It is critical to understand that not all autistic people are the same. We know that there are many subtypes of autism, most of which are influenced by a combination of genetic and environmental factors.

People with autism learn, think, and solve problems in a variety of ways, ranging from highly skilled to severely challenged. Because autism is a spectrum disorder, each autistic person has a unique set of strengths and challenges.

Some people with ASD may require significant assistance in their daily lives, whereas others may require less assistance and, in some cases, live completely independently. Early intervention, according to research, leads to better outcomes for people with autism later in life.

Note from the Publisher

Autism is often accompanied by sensory sensitivities and medical issues such as gastrointestinal (GI) disorders, seizures, or sleep disorders, as well as mental health challenges such as anxiety, depression, and attention issues. Some people exhibit all symptoms, while others exhibit only a few, and still others may have most of their symptoms under control to the point where you can't tell they have autism.

Because every person is unique, no single statement about autism can be universally true. However, most autistic people struggle to express their emotions. This is not to say that an autistic person does not have feelings. He or she simply cannot express how he or she feels. It also does not rule out the possibility of strong interpersonal bonds. Contrary to popular belief, many autistic people are happily married and in love. Most people find it more difficult to form relationships, but it is possible to do so over time.

The most important characteristics to remember are compassion and tolerance. You will almost certainly need to be patient when dealing with autistic people but knowing a little more about the disorder may make this easier.

Learn what you can and share your knowledge with those you know to help create a more accepting environment in your community for autistic people.

- Deedra Abboud, & Tara Ijai

Introduction

I had gone to dinner with Yahya and his family as I often do, this time for my birthday, and Yahya's mom, Sue, prompted Yahya to show me the book he was writing about his life with *The Wiggles*. As I read his first ten pages, I was impressed with his writing as well as the fact that he had written it completely on his phone – something I could never have done.

I turned to Sue and asked how she planned to publish it. She replied that they planned to just print it out and staple it together. Yahya wanted to share it with all his friends. I told her we could publish it for real if they were interested.

When she asked Yahya, he became very excited.

At one point Yahya asked if his "real" published book could be listed on *Amazon*, and he got really excited when I explained that "real" publishing meant his book would be listed on book websites like *Amazon*.

Yahya was a little disappointed when he found out the book couldn't be published by Christmas, only a few weeks away, but his excitement bounced back quickly when I agreed his book could be published by Valentine's Day.

A few weeks later, Sue sent me Yahya's finished manuscript. As my first step in editing, I ran the file through a plagiarism checker. Despite all the biographical information about the Wiggles characters, every sentence in the book was original to Yahya. Again, I was impressed.

Beyond a few added commas, paragraph separations, italics for building names, chapter divisions, and chapter titles, the only changes I suggested for Yahya's approval were additional descriptions of the characters, like adding that Dorothy was the Dinosaur, for people like myself who weren't familiar with the Wiggles characters.

I sent Yahya a series of personal questions, which he answered right away, and then I asked him to turn his answers to four of the questions into his closing chapter.

And that's how this book by an autistic boy describing his adventures with The Wiggles around the world for two decades came to be.

Discovering The Wiggles

My name is Yahya Lutfi. I am 28 years old, and I have autism. I like music and dancing and I love to travel. When I was young, I watched the typical children's shows such as *Thomas the Tank Engine, Blue's Clues*, *Barney*, and *Captain Kangaroo.* One day in 1997, while I was watching *Mr. Moose's Fun Time*, on Fox Family channel, they showed a one-song clip of four guys singing and dancing to a very upbeat and fun song. I was mesmerized. Who were these guys?

This continued to be a regular feature on that show and the only clue I had was when they introduced the segment, Captain Kangaroo said, "It's Wiggle time!" What did that mean? Did it refer to the dancing? Was it somehow connected to the name of the guys? Well, I never did find out and the next year, in 1998, this segment was no longer on *Mr. Moose's Fun Time* show. I missed seeing "Wiggle time" but soon discovered that there was show called

"Wiggle House" on Fox Family channel. I was so happy to see them back but still didn't know who they were. So, I went to the internet.

I discovered *The Wiggles* were from Sydney, NSW, Australia, and they changed my life forever. They are Murray Cook, Jeff Fatt, Anthony Field, and Greg Page. Before *The Wiggles*, these guys were in rock bands in Sydney in the 1970s. Murray was in a band called *Finger Guns* and then *Bang Shang a Lang*. Greg was in a band called *Dead Giveaway* while he was still in high school. Jeff was in a band called the *Road Masters* with his brothers, and Anthony and his brother Paul started a band called the *Cockroaches*. They asked Jeff to join them, and Greg became a roadie for them. They were very successful throughout Australia for many years. They wrote many of their own songs and had four hit albums in the late 1980s to early 1990s. They were described as the hardest working rock'n'roll band in the country by the *Daily Telegraph*, playing 300 gigs a year.

Then tragedy struck when Paul's newborn daughter died of SIDS (sudden infant death syndrome) while the *Cockroaches* were on the road. Paul was devastated and the *Cockroaches* eventually broke up.

As they thought about what to do next, Anthony decided to go to Macquarie University to study early childhood education and become a pre-school teacher. Coincidentally, Greg and Murray also decided to study to be pre-school teachers at the university.

At the university, Anthony learned about child development, child psychology, how children think, and the importance of play in the children's lives. He loved all the courses. Murray Cook, Greg Page and Anthony also jammed together, along with a few other musicians at the university. Anthony would frequently invite his brother John (who was also a member of the *Cockroaches*) to join them for these lunchtime sessions. They had so much fun jamming together that they decided to try busking (entertaining on the streets of Sydney) with coins occasionally being thrown into Greg's guitar case. Jeff Fatt, another member of the *Cockroaches*, was called up by Anthony to play the accordion for the busking group. So, this group without a name, but with their knowledge of early childhood education and a growing number of songs, took their first step towards success.

They needed a name. Anthony's brother John wrote a song for them called "Get Ready to Wiggle." Anthony noted that was how they wanted the children to dance – to wiggle – and they had their name – *The Wiggles.* So, in 1991, Anthony decided to record an album of children's music based on concepts he learned in his studies of early childhood education. He asked Murray Cook and Greg Page as well as a fellow classmate, Phillip Wilcher, to be a part of this and called an old friend, Jeff Fatt, to join them too. Jeff asked how long it would take as he had some other projects and Anthony said "don't know – maybe a couple of hours" – and thus *The Wiggles* were born and are still going strong 30 years later, although

Phillip decided to leave the group after the first album, "The Wiggles" was recorded in August 1991.

The Wiggles signed with ABC Music and began touring Australia. They performed in schools, shopping centers, parks, birthday parties, and just about anywhere else that they could. They were becoming more and more popular. They released another album and decided to use solid-colored skivvies rather than the shirts used in their first two albums. They each picked their favorite color – Murray was red, Jeff was purple, Greg was yellow, and Anthony was green. Anthony later changed to blue.

As I said, I saw one-song clips of *The Wiggles* in 1997 on the *Captain Kangaroo* show and then the next year, they had their "Wiggle House" show on Fox Family. It was time for *The Wiggles* to make a name for themselves outside of Australia.

In 1999, *The Wiggles* went to Disneyland. I wish I had heard about that. They performed in Fantasyland.

In 2000, they were signed by Lyrick Studios (home of *Barney*). Lyrick Studios released the first *Wiggles* album here in America and called it "Let's Wiggle" (this is actually the same album released in Australia which was called "Wiggle Time").

In 2001, *The Wiggles* struck the big time in the US. They toured with the *Barney's Musical Castle* show as an intermission act. I was so excited! By coincidence, my mom had bought tickets for us to see this *Barney* show and then to find out that the act I have been waiting to see for years was going to be performing also, I was over the moon!

Well as things turned out, *The Wiggles* started the tour in Dallas in mid-September and performed with *Barney* in seven cities (just a little over a month) and then left the tour just before they were to come to Phoenix, so I didn't get to see them. I was very disappointed.

Starstruck

In 2002, *The Wiggles* toured the US on their own. They were coming to Phoenix! They would be playing at the *Celebrity Theater* on June 2, 2002. It was a dream come true! We got our tickets, and I couldn't wait. I was 8 when I finally got to meet these amazing men.

Anthony Field (the blue Wiggle) had some teeth problems and was not able to be there in Phoenix, although he did join the tour later. His brother Paul wore the blue skivvy and performed at the Phoenix show.

In those days, the Wiggles themselves jumped on and off the stage to interact with the audience and to collect roses for Dorothy the Dinosaur. As it was my first concert, I didn't know that people brought roses for Dorothy, and I didn't bring any, but as Murray was passing us, he stopped to greet us.

My mom told him how much I loved *The Wiggles*, that I was autistic and asked if it would be at all possible to actually meet them after the show. Murray said he would ask the other guys and when he went back on the stage, he kept pointing to me and talking to each one. Then a security guard came up to us and told us to wait in our seats after the show and he would take us backstage.

They were waiting for us when we got backstage. I sat at a table with them and just stared, a little starstruck, I guess. I had waited more than five years for this moment!

Yahya listening to the 'Five Little Ducks' song.

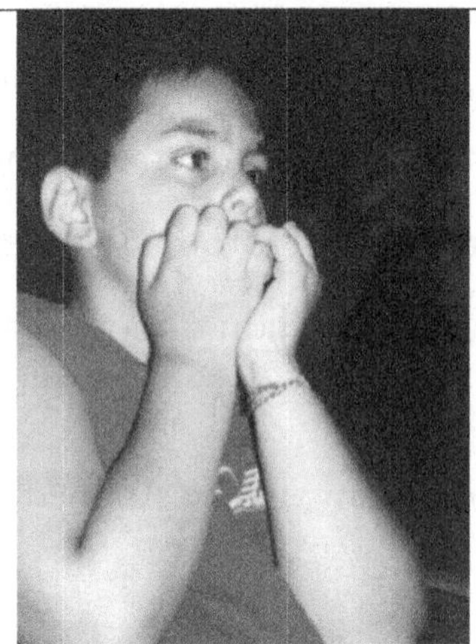

When I was young, I was very quiet, not non-verbal but I didn't talk a lot. My mom stood back while I was with the Wiggles, each of them talking to me and asking me questions, but I didn't answer anyone. Then, Jeff (the purple Wiggle) asked me something. I think he asked me how old I was, and I answered him. After that, I just talked to the guys and answered their questions. My mom took some pictures, and you could see how happy I was. Usually in pictures, I just gave a little smile, but this time I was just glowing with happiness.

It Begins: Yahya with The Wiggles.

Jeff (purple Wiggle) and Yahya.

My mom sent a copy of the pictures to *The Wiggles'* office in Australia, thanking them for taking the time to meet me, and to show how happy it made me.

A few weeks later, we got an envelope from Australia. It was a letter from Paul Field, *The Wiggles'* manager, thanking her for the letter and lovely photos and saying how pleased he was that my meeting with *The Wiggles* was so memorable. He said that "Meeting their fans is one of *The Wiggles* most enjoyable times too." He also included 8-1/2 x 11-inch poster personally signed for me by all the Wiggles as well as their friends, Dorothy (the Dinosaur), Henry (the Octopus), Wags (the Dog), and the Captain (Feathersword, "the friendly pirate"). It was one of the best gifts I have ever received.

Back in the days before Facebook, *The Wiggles* had a message board where fans could chat, occasionally a Wiggle might respond to a question or chat, you could get the latest news about upcoming concerts, merchandise, and other important information. A lot of the fans became on-line friends, sometimes even meeting up at concerts.

The Wiggles also had a magazine that was published during these years. It had coloring pages, stories and news about *The Wiggles,* games, and a fan mail section where they printed letters, pictures, and artwork sent in by fans. A short time after my mom sent the pictures of me to *The Wiggles,* Colleen who was one of our *Wiggles Message Board* friends, asked if that was me in newest issue of *The Wiggles* magazine. My mom asked what she was talking about, and she sent us a copy of the picture in the magazine.

Yahya & Greg (yellow Wiggle)

Well, sure enough, it was me! What a surprise! It was the picture of Greg and me with a caption something like "Greg meets a friend in Phoenix,

Arizona." I ordered a bunch of that issue to give to my relatives and friends!

I saw that *The Wiggles* were playing in Minneapolis and Madison in August and my mom told me that if I could behave and not have any tantrums or meltdowns, and do everything I was told, she would take me to those shows.

I couldn't believe it. I was going to see them two more times! I was on my best behavior for the next two months and we were off to see *The Wiggles* again.

We flew into Milwaukee and on August 17th, we drove up to Minneapolis to see *The Wiggles* at the *Minnesota Historic State Theater.* It was a long drive, but I didn't complain. I was too excited! On the drive up, my mom had found a store that sold *Wiggles* items. She stopped and bought me a couple of new CDs for the ride. We also stopped and got Dorothy some roses.

At intermission, we saw Jeff (the purple Wiggle) taking his bike out for a ride before the second show and we talked to him for a few minutes.

Jeff (purple Wiggle)

After the second (last) show, we saw Greg (the yellow Wiggle) leaving and managed to talk to him for a few minutes, but he was in a hurry. He is a huge Elvis fan, and he was headed to the airport to go see Graceland for a day.

Yahya and Greg (yellow Wiggle)

We left to go back to Milwaukee. The Madison concerts were August 19th. We drove up to Madison to see *The Wiggles* again at the *Oscar Mayer Theater.* Our seats were excellent and there was a pretty good-sized crowd. After the last show, everyone was waiting at the tour buses for the guys to come out.

In those days, they met and talked to people at their bus. I saw Murray (the red Wiggle) and when I went up to him, he said "I know you. I think I met you in Phoenix."

Yahya and Murray (red Wiggle)

Yes! I was completely amazed that having only met them once a show in a different city and over two months ago, that he could remember me! I told him yes, I live in Phoenix, and I met them after the show in Phoenix.

I then went up to Greg and he was with a small group of younger kids. It was hot out and he had the sleeves of his skivvy pushed up to his elbows. Being autistic, I also have sensory problems and one of my issues is that it bothers me to have short sleeves, I always wear long sleeves. Well, I saw the sleeves of his skivvy were pushed up and I walked up to the group of kids and proceeded to pull his sleeves down. He looked at me, laughed and said, "Okay if you don't like them up, we will keep them down." Then after the younger kids left, I went up to talk to him. I told him "I'm Yahya" and he said, "Yes I think I met you in Phoenix, right?" Again, I was amazed that they remembered me.

Then I went up to Anthony (the blue Wiggle). Since I hadn't met him before, I wasn't sure what to say. My mom had to prompt me. So, I introduced myself. I said, "I'm Yahya" and he responded, "Good to meet you Yahya."

Yahya and Anthony (blue Wiggle)

I told him I hadn't met him, but I did meet his brother Paul in Phoenix when he filled in for Anthony. Then I asked him without any prompting where Paul was and he said, "Paul went home to Australia." I said, "Okay, Paul is home in Australia" and walked away.

I then saw Anthony walk over to a teenager with Down's syndrome who was standing away from the crown and start talking to him. I thought to myself these are the most amazing people.

Yahya and Jeff (purple Wiggle)

Yahya and Jeff (purple Wiggle)

Yahya and Paul Paddick (Captain Featherword)

Yahya and Ben Murray (dancer)

They Treated *Me* Like The Star!

In 2003, *The Wiggles* toured the US again. This time, I had seats in the first row at *ASU Gammage Auditorium.* They saw me immediately when they came on stage. While they took a few moments to read signs that everyone brought, they said they would like to introduce a good friend who was at the concert today and they asked me to stand up and take a bow. Everyone clapped for me. It felt good that they still remembered me and acknowledge me like that.

That year, Greg had to miss the concert because of a family emergency, and it was Sam Moran's first performance as the yellow Wiggle. Sam did stop and say "hi" while he was off stage collecting roses. He seemed very nice.

I didn't go to the second show this time, but my friend Kim did. She also had front row seats and totally enjoyed the show.

At the end, as the curtain was closing, her mom asked Murray if they could meet the guys and Murray said that unfortunately they had to pack up fast and leave right away. Her mom then said, "I know Yahya" and Murray stopped, turned and said, "You know Yahya – well maybe I can get a couple of the guys together and do a very short meeting." To me that was the ultimate compliment – to treat me like the star and meet my friend!

That summer, I again went out of town to see *The Wiggles.* I went to St. Louis and saw them at the *Fox Theater.* Anthony missed this show because he had to have surgery and was back in Australia. Brett Clarke, one of the Wiggly dancers, was taking Anthony's place as the blue Wiggle for this show. The other three Wiggles saw me from stage and waved but I didn't have a chance to talk to them this time. I did take my chocolate roses for Dorothy up to the stage and handed them to Brett. I always brought chocolate roses because I thought those would taste better than real roses or plastic roses. After the show, we went sightseeing in St. Louis. We saw the Gateway Arch. That was really cool!

In 2003, *The Wiggles* decided to branch out and introduced the *Taiwanese Wiggles.* The original *Taiwanese Wiggles* lineup was Danny as the purple Wiggle, James Arthur as the blue Wiggle, Carlos as the yellow Wiggle, and Annie as the red Wiggle. Annie was the first female Wiggle. The *Taiwanese Wiggles* were disbanded in 2007 as they did not catch on, but you can still see them on *YouTube.* They are really fun to watch.

In the spring of 2003, Greg Page had a solo concert in Las Vegas at the Stardust Hotel with the *TCB Band* (they were Elvis' backup band). I heard that a lot of our *Wiggles Message Board* friends traveled to Las Vegas for the show, but we didn't go. After the show, Greg came out and talked to them. He did another show in Nashville in July of 2004. Greg is a huge Elvis Presley fan who owns the world's fourth-largest collection of Elvis Presley memorabilia, which includes clothing, a marriage certificate, a guitar, a piano, Elvis' final Cadillac, and original *TCB Band* necklaces. In 2008, Page donated his collection, reportedly worth $1.5 million, to a new Elvis Museum in Parkes, New South Wales.

A Special Bond

The Wiggles performed at the *Dodge Theater* in Phoenix on April 28, 2004. By this time, the touring manager had set up a regularly scheduled meet-and-greet for kids with special needs. They took about 5-10 families into the auditorium early and had everyone sit in the first couple of rows of the theater, then Anthony, Jeff, Murray, Greg, and Captain Feathersword would go from family to family to say "hi" and take a quick picture.

They always came to me last because then they were able to spend more than a minute or two chatting while my mom took several pictures.

Yahya and Wiggles

Sometimes I also brought things for them to autograph, which they did even though they said no autographs were allowed.

Paul Field taking my Wiggles dolls to be autographed.

This became pretty much the norm as far as meetings for the next several years but that was okay because I always got to talk to them.

Sam Moran (dancer) and Yahya.

On December 26, 2004, Indonesia suffered an earthquake of a magnitude of 9 with many resultant tsunamis which devastated the entire country. An estimated 212,000 or more deaths and 6,245 missing occurred. The world banded together and sent help to Indonesia. *The Wiggles* also wanted to help and on January 29, 2005, the Cockroaches reunited for the "Hills for Hope" concert as a benefit for the tsunami survivors. Also playing were the Greg Page Band, Mental As Anything, and Hush. They also sold "Hills for Hope" t-shirts at the concert and on *The Wiggles Message Board.* Many of their fans bought them through the *Message Board.* Both my mom and I bought one.

“Hey Yahya!” In London

In 2005, *The Wiggles* again came to Phoenix, on April 8-9th at the *Dodge Theater.* I was again included in the before-the-show meet and greet for special needs kids, and got to chat with them before the show, being the last person who they greeted. *The Wiggles* were touring the US every year and it was fun to see them so often.

Yahya giving chocolate roses to Greg on stage.

It had been a while since I had traveled to another city to see them. They were to perform in London at the *Apollo Hammersmith Theater* on July 11-12, 2005. I was so excited when my mom told me that we could go to London to see them! I had never been to London, and I was going to see my favorite people in the world. But would they recognize me in another country? That was really a long way from where they were used to seeing me.

As I was walking around outside the venue before the second show, I heard someone say, "Hey Yahya!" I turned around to see Anthony, who had just stepped outside for a breath of air before the second show. I couldn't believe that he recognized me from the back, in a totally different country. These guys are amazing, and they are exactly what they seemed to be, caring and compassionate.

Anthony and Yahya.

I brought my "Hills for Hope" t-shirt along and asked him if all the guys would sign it. He asked if I wanted Paul to sign it and I said "of course, he was a member of the Cockroaches." Then he asked if I wanted Greg to sign it and I said, "I would like whoever was there to sign it and Greg was there." He said he would, and he would give it to Al-Pal at the sound board and I could pick it up after the show.

Yahya in London.

London was great. We went to a play in the West End, saw all the tourist spots. We went on the London Eye. That was great! I love Ferris Wheels. We went shopping at the famous toy shop, Hamleys (that was such an amazing place).

Hamleys London: Yahya with Harry Potter & Hagrid made in Legos.

I bought something called ghost bubbles. They are so cool. You shoot the bubble gun and bubbles emerge, and then they just disappear like a puff of smoke, like a ghost.

And we attended two awesome *Wiggles* shows.

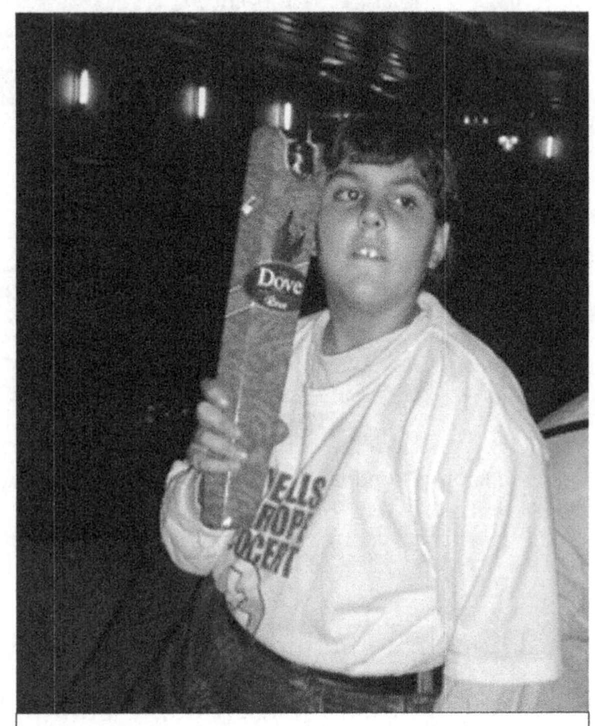

Yahya carrying chocolate roses for Dorothy.

Yahya and Wiggles.

"Hey Yahya!" in London

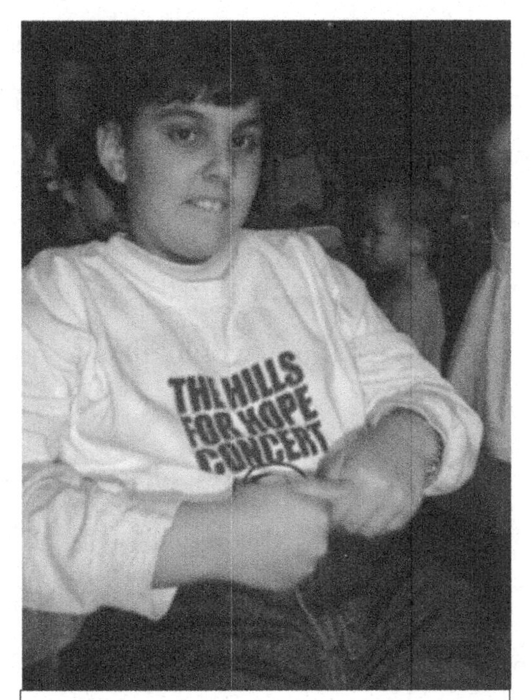

Yahya wearing 'The Hills for Hope Concert' Fundraiser shirt.

Yahya with Wiggles.

In 2005, *The Wiggles* premiered the *Latin American Wiggles* on Latin American TV Show in Mexico City called "The Wiggles Show." Anthony called his old friend Fernando Monguel, whom he had met when touring with the *Barney's Musical Castle* in 2001 and asked if he would like to join the *Latin American Wiggles.* The *Latin American Wiggles* are Fernando as the yellow Wiggle, Katty as the purple Wiggle, Francisco as the red Wiggle, and Zoe as the blue Wiggle. Although the show aired on Disney Channel Latin America in 2006, no official CDs or DVDs featuring the group were ever released. However, you can now see them on *YouTube.*

More Bonding

The Wiggles were back at the *Dodge Theater* in Phoenix for their 15th birthday celebration show on April 29-30, 2006, when I was 13 years old. It was a special show.

I was included in the usual pre-show meet-and-greet. I brought them a special gift, a CD by another friend of mine, Dawud Wharnsby, a Canadian Universalist Muslim singer-songwriter, poet, performer, educator, and television personality. It was called "Sunshine, Dust and the Messenger." This is my favorite CD of his. I told them my favorite song on this CD was "Rhythm of Surrender." Dawud sings Islamic children's songs, which are called nasheeds. *The Wiggles* were excited to listen to it, and Anthony said he would share it with his sister Anne Field, who is Muslim.

I also found out that *The Wiggles* were going to be in London again and I would get to go again! We flew into London, on July 12, 2006, and we took the train to Brighton for our first *UK Wiggles* show. We walked around the town before the show. We saw Brighton Pier where there were carnival rides and games. It was kind of like Santa Monica Pier in California.

When it was time for the show, we went to the venue and found our seats. *The Wiggles* came out on stage and were so surprised to see me. After greeting the crowd, they said, "We have a special friend in the audience today who came all the way from Phoenix, Arizona in the US to see us – Yahya will you stand and take a bow?"

Yahya with Wiggles before show.

Yahya with Brett Clarke (dancer).

On July 13-14, 2006, *The Wiggles* had two shows at the *Apollo Hammersmith Theater.* There were no meet-and-greets in London, but I did hand my chocolate roses for Dorothy directly to Anthony on the stage instead of having them collected. I met a lot of *The Wiggles Message Board* friends at these two UK concerts.

We also again went to a play in the West End. It was *Footloose* and it was awesome – that is my favorite movie and I performed in it in a children's theater group, but the live version of it was better than anything I could imagine!

In November 2006, Greg surprised *The Wiggles'* world by announcing that he was diagnosed with Orthostatic Intolerance which means his heart doesn't pump blood all around his body. He was feeling ill for a long time, feeling dizzy when he got up too fast, and feeling like he wasn't able to perform as well as he used to. After many tests, many visits to doctors, and many trial treatments, he was diagnosed with Orthostatic Intolerance. The treatment was for him not to do as much physical activity and sadly, he made the decision to leave *The Wiggles* for his health. He passed the yellow skivvy to Sam Moran on December 5, 2006, and Sam was the yellow Wiggle from 2007 to 2011.

“Getting Strong” In All The Ways

In 2007, *The Wiggles* opened their new studio, *Hot Potato Studios.* This was to be where all their new videos and albums were going to be made. The first album they made at their new studio was “Getting Strong.”

The Wiggles returned to Phoenix on March 8, 2007, and I had the best time at the concert. I was included in the pre-show meet and greet.

Yahya with Wiggles.

I had been learning Photoshop in school and I made a welcome card for Sam, which I gave to him at the meet and greet. Instead of a regular rose for Dorothy, this year I brought a helium balloon rose and this time I gave it to Murray when he passed around to collect roses.

How I Have Grown

In 2008, *The Wiggles* decided to use a larger venue and we had to drive out to *Cardinals Stadium* in Glendale, Arizona. It was a long drive, and the venue was too big for much interaction, but it was fun anyway.

As always, I was included in the pre-show meet-and-greet, and this year, I made a collage of pictures from all the previous pictures I had taken with them from when I first met them until that year. An individual one for each Wiggle (and one for Greg which Anthony promised he would give to him). I titled it "How I have grown."

Yahya with Wiggles.

He Said, "Leave Us Alone"

The Wiggles returned to the *Dodge Theater* on July 27, 2009. Again, they had their pre-show meet-and-greet in which I was included. As always, we were the last group they talked to, and I gave them some "Phoenix Zoo Walk" t-shirts and an Autism Awareness car magnet. They asked me a lot of questions about the "Phoenix Zoo Walk" like how long it had been going on, and how big was it, and then they put the Autism Awareness magnet on the Big Red Car so everyone could see it when they drove onto the stage.

On July 25, 2010, *The Wiggles* decided to do something different. They were performing at the *Diamondbacks Baseball Stadium* after the game. So, we bought a ticket to the game, and I wondered how this was going to work.

After everyone left the stadium and only the families who wanted to see the concert were left, security called everyone who was to get a meet-and-greet. This time *The Wiggles* did something different. Instead of having a meet-and-greet for special needs kids, apparently, they had some kind of radio contest to win a meet-and-greet with *The Wiggles.* So besides me, there were about 10 kids, all of whom were there because they had won the contest.

I took my usual place at the end of the line. Everyone got only a few seconds each, not even time for a picture before the security guard hurried them out. When I got my turn, I gave them a framed picture that I made with Photoshop, a cartoon of five Wiggles on a stage –Murray, Jeff, Sam, Anthony, and me in a Wiggles costume as the "green Wiggle." We were talking and a security guard came up and told us that we had to go. Anthony told him to leave us alone, that we were talking.

Yahya with Wiggles.

The Audition Tape

In 2011, *The Wiggles* had been touring all over the world for 20 years! They released a special Wiggly birthday album and video called "Big Birthday." As a special surprise for fans, *The Wiggles* announced a competition. If you won, you would go up on stage and sing and dance with the Wiggles when they sang fruit salad. This was my dream come true! If only I could win the contest. For every city that they toured in 2011, there would be a winner. Unfortunately, *The Wiggles* didn't come to Phoenix in 2011. They were, however, going to be in Chicago and I sent in my competition video for that city.

It was time to make my video. I wrote an introduction speech, choreographed my dance steps, and rehearsed the song. One of my old *Childsplay Theater* teachers, Jodi, helped me.

According to the rules of the competition, the fans on the *Wiggles Message Board* would vote for the best video. However, the Wiggles would make the final decision. Fans could vote for one contestant once a day and whoever had the most votes would win. Jodi videotaped my song and we uploaded it to the competition site. My mom posted on T*he Wiggles Message Board* asking if all her friends could vote for me to help me win. All those great people voted for me!

There was only one other person competing in the Chicago contest. I had way more votes than him and thought for sure I would win. However, the day before the contest ended, someone posted a video. I don't know how they got any votes since their post was last minute, but they won the contest. They did have a great costume and great props, though, and they were announced as the winner. I was sad but you never know when another opportunity might come along. So, I didn't go to Chicago that year and didn't see *The Wiggles* that year. If you are curious, you can see my competition video on *YouTube* if you search for "Phoenix Yahya Wiggle."

Scary news again rocked the Wiggly world. In early July 2011, Jeff was experiencing heart problems and was diagnosed as having a heart arrhythmia. That is an irregular heartbeat, either beating too slow or beating too fast. He had been feeling unwell for several weeks and then had a blackout while driving. Fortunately, neither Jeff nor anyone else was hurt. He underwent heart surgery and was fitted with a defibrillator and was expected to recover completely. He had never missed a show in the 20 years of touring but because of this, he missed the summer US tour.

A New Wiggles Lineup

Great news! In 2012, Greg returned to *The Wiggles* and Sam was no longer in *The Wiggles*! Then the sad news. On May 17, 2012, *The Wiggles* announced that Jeff, Murray, and Greg would retire from *The Wiggles* at the end of the Celebration Tour.

The Wiggles returned to Phoenix on July 24, 2012, back at the *Comerica Theater.* At the pre-show meet-and-greet, there was a very small group. We spent a lot of time talking to all the guys, wishing them well, and telling them how much they would be missed. I photoshopped note cards for each of them with a picture of the Sydney Harbour Bridge with them and me sitting in front of it. Armed with my chocolate rose and a Frisbee for Wags, I enjoyed a great show and Lachy (who was a dancer at that time) walked through the audience collecting the roses.

The rest of the 2012 tour passed quickly and soon it was time for three of the four Wiggles who started this ground-breaking children's band to retire. What would retirement be like for these three guys who have been touring the world for 20+ years, doing maybe 50 or more shows per year? Would they just lay back and relax?

No, that was not the way these guys are. They had too much energy and loved entertaining people too much. Murray was in a band called *Bang Shang A Lang* since the 1980s and he was out playing with them whenever he was not touring overseas with *The Wiggles.* After he retired from *The Wiggles*, he re-joined *Bang Shang A Lang* full time and played at various venues all around Sydney.

Greg, on the other hand, stayed in the children's entertainment industry. He was doing a show called *Butterscotch's Playground.* I really liked this show. Greg would interact with a puppet named Butterscotch, who is a bunny, and his three friends, Frankie who is a monkey, Honey Bear who is a bear, and Charles who is a bird. They go on adventures around the world. It teaches children to be curious and to learn about their surroundings. They also show the kids how to turn the entire world into a giant playground. They go places like a fire station, they visit a dance studio, and learn the history of baseball, to name a few adventures. You can see clips of *Butterscotch's Playground* on *YouTube.*

Jeff did this and that. I heard he was involved behind the scenes with *The Wiggles.* He participated in the *Cockroaches* reunion shows, and also joined the *Sacred Hearts* reunion shows. The *Sacred Hearts* are a Rockabilly band comprised of members of the *Cockroaches.* [Rockabilly music originated in the early 1950s in the United States, particularly in the South. As a genre, it combines the sounds of Western musical styles such as country with rhythm and blues, resulting in what is known as "classic" rock and roll.]

It was really fun listening to their music and one day I would love to see both the *Cockroaches* and the *Sacred Hearts.*

Now the new Wiggles were ready to go. Simon Pryce was replacing Murray as the red Wiggle. Lachy Gillespie replaced Jeff as the purple Wiggle, and an announcement that rocked the Wiggle world, Emma Watkins replaced Greg as the yellow Wiggle. Emma was the first female (Australian) Wiggle. Would *The Wiggles* be different with a new lineup? How would having a female Wiggle affect the group?

And So I Danced

Another milestone in 2013. On May 23, 2013, I graduated from high school.

My high school graduation picture.

My high school graduation party cake.

Although I loved dancing since I was little, in high school I began taking dance classes, both at school and private lessons. I participated in all the shows at school and learned how to do choreography. I also participated with several of the children's theaters here.

'Annie' - Ahwatukee Children's Theater 2013

'Shrek' - Detour Theater 2015.

Maricopa County Community College (MCC) Dance Show 2019.

One of my private dance teachers, Emmy, received an offer for some of her students to dance at one of the music stages at the *Arizona State Fair.* I was so excited but at the last minute, for unknown reasons, our show was cancelled. That was a big disappointment, but I will continue dancing.

I got to talk to everyone before the show on September 11, 2013 at the *Comerica Theater.* The new Wiggles seemed somewhat shy, but they were very easy to talk to. Emma was very sweet and really easy to talk to. Simon and Lachy were also very friendly. This group worked very well together. I knew that these new Wiggles would be great. The show was more than enjoyable. It was different but the same!

Yahya with Wiggles and Nick Hutchinson (dancer).

Yahya with Nick Hutchinson (dancer).

A Surprise Down Under

On June 14, 2014, to celebrate the release of their album catalog on *iTunes*, the *Cockroaches* decided to reunite for two reunion concerts. For the first time in over 25 years, Paul Field (lead vocals), Anthony Field (lead guitar), Jeff Fatt (keyboards), Tony Henry (drums), Paul Dunworth (bass), and John Field (guitar) played together.

In 2014, when *The Wiggles* released their third nursery rhymes album and video, called "Apples and Bananas," Wiggles fans got an unexpected surprise. Everyone knew everyone from *The Wiggles Message Board*, as I mentioned, so we were all surprised and delighted to learn that Anthony had contacted someone from our group, Linda, whose daughter Baylee was a huge Wiggles fan and also a great dancer. He asked if Baylee would like to dance in the "Fa La Ninna" song on the "Apples and Bananas" video.

She was 14 at the time they started filming and she was amazing. It was so great that they chose someone who was a fan, and someone well known to the Wiggles' fans rather than an unknown professional dancer.

The Wiggles did not return to Phoenix in 2014 but I got the best news in the world. My mom told me that we were going to visit Australia in 2015!

Australia Bound

Before we left for Australia, I had seen an advertisement that Dargie Entertainment was looking for new dancers and the auditions would be in January 2016. The Director of Dargie Entertainment was Ben Murray who had been a dancer with *The Wiggles* and someone I had met many times. He left *The Wiggles* in 2005. Being a dancer was my dream-come-true, so I prepared a resume and audition tape to send to him. I explained that I was coming from the US and would be in Australia only until just before Christmas. I told him we had met several times and asked if he remembered me. I didn't receive an answer, but I thought that it might be a problem hiring someone who wasn't an Australian citizen or maybe because I couldn't be there for the actual auditions. Well, better luck next time for me.

I left for Australia on November 29, 2015. I couldn't be more excited! I had plans to see and do everything that there was to do. I was 22 years old and had plans to see all the Wiggles, especially the ones who had new bands.

Our flight from Phoenix to LA was delayed which meant that we had to run across the terminal to catch our connecting flight in LA. I got separated from my parents and got lost trying to find the gate. Luckily my mother found me, and we got to the plane in the nick of time. We were on our way to Australia! After crossing the International Date Line, which added a day to our travel, we arrived in Brisbane on December 1, 2015.

Our hotel view on Sunshine Coast.

We settled into our hotel, the Wharf Boutique Apartments in Surfer's Paradise, Queensland. After a quick nap, we went out exploring the area. The first thing I noticed about Australia was that the cars drove on the wrong side of the street.

In the US, of course, we look left, right, left before we cross the street. In Australia, you have to look right, left, right and then cross. It was difficult to remember. They even had it written at the cross walks "look right, left, right before you cross."

We then went to *Aussie World* for a couple of hours. *Aussie World* is a small amusement park with rides, mini golf, and they had some local groups performing Christmas songs and dancing with the audience, even inviting the audience on stage to dance with them. That was the best part of *Aussie World.*

Yahya dancing on-stage at Aussie World.

After a good night's sleep, we went to the Eumundi Markets in Eumundi, Queensland the next day. That place was awesome! It was like the whole city was a farmer's market/craft market. They had everything you could dream of, over 600 exhibitors.

Then we went to the Sunshine Plaza Mall in Surfer's Paradise to look around. That place was bigger than any mall I have seen here in the US.

Sunshine Plaza Shopping Centre.

They had a food court that was next to a lake. They had some fast-food places in Australia but not too many. They had just recently gotten McDonalds, and everyone thought that was the best place ever! They also had a Burger King, but they called it Hungry Jacks. I think they also had boat rides around the river! Who would have thought? The next day we would be visiting the Australia Zoo.

The day had finally come. We were going to Steve Irwin's Zoo. Steve Irwin was the famous Australian "Crocodile Hunter." That is the best zoo I have ever visited. There were many opportunities to interact with the animals and a lot of animal shows. I saw a crocodile feeding show where the handlers walked right up to the crocs to feed them. I held a koala and saw and petted many other animals. The kangaroos and wallabies were roaming free, and you could just walk up to them and pet them.

Tiger feeding at Australia Zoo: Home of the Crocodile Hunter.

Yahya holding a koala.

Yahya feeding a Australian white cockatoo.

Yahya and dad petting a snake.

The following day, we went to *Currumbin Wildlife Sanctuary*. This was smaller than the Australia Zoo but just as nice. We walked through the Sanctuary. Kangaroos and wallabies were again roaming free. I even saw a kangaroo with a baby in her pouch! They had an area where you could hold animals. I wanted to hold a crocodile, but they had just closed the crocodile exhibit when we got there.

Yahya feeding wallaby.

The fun continues! This was our last day in Queensland, and we were going to *Dreamworld* on the

Gold Coast. This is the largest theme park in Australia with over 40 rides and attractions. They had some great roller coasters. I love roller coasters!

Yahya at Dreamworld.

In *Wiggle World* in *Dreamland*, there was a Wiggles show (not the real Wiggles) but it was fun, nevertheless. I saw Dorothy the Dinosaur's Beach Party and sang and danced along with the kids and the cast!

Yahya at Wiggle World.

Yahya with "Dorothy" at Wiggle World.

Yahya with Henry at Wiggle World.

On December 6th, we left Queensland and flew to Sydney. We got settled in our hotel, the Sydney Harbour Marriott Hotel at Circular Quay, and went out sightseeing. We saw the Sydney Harbour Bridge and the Sydney Opera House.

Sydney Opera House.

Yahya at gift shop inside Sydney Opera House.

We explored the inside of the Sydney Opera House and took a ferry over to Darling Harbour to explore the shops and restaurants.

Yahya at Darling Harbor.

Yahya at Hard Rock Café, Sydney.

Just as we went into a restaurant for dinner, a big rainstorm came up. Rain was pouring down really hard, and the wind was blowing. The thunder and lightning were almost constant. Most of the restaurants in the area had open fronts (no door or front wall/windows) and the wind was blowing tablecloths off the empty tables and people sitting near the front were getting soaked and their food was being blown all over. Everyone huddled near the back of the restaurant until the storm passed. I never saw that big of a storm. Where I live in Phoenix, we barely get any rain. It actually was pretty fun. It finally mostly stopped, and we went back to ferry to go back to our hotel.

The next day, we went to Sydney's *Powerhouse Museum* where they have a fantastic exhibit of Wiggles memorabilia. They had a big red car, skivvies, guitars, the Wiggle House, and a short history of the Wiggles.

They also had a lot of other exhibits too. They also had an awesome *Legos* exhibit of superheroes.

They even had the *Lost in Space* Robot (do you remember him – "Danger, Will Robinson").

Yahya with 'Lost in Space" robot.

On December 8th, we were going to go stand-up paddle boarding at Tony Henry's Stand-Up Paddle in Avalon. Tony Henry was the drummer for the *Cockroaches* and when they disbanded, he opened a stand-up paddle boarding business.

The previous evening, my mom contacted Paul Field to get directions on how to get there and Paul asked when we were going to go and said that he and some of the guys might be able to meet us there. She said tomorrow and Paul said that unfortunately they wouldn't be able to go until Wednesday. Well, we had other plans on Wednesday so that didn't work for us, and we were not able to meet up.

When we got to Tony's place, I had my lesson with his son Theo. We stayed out about an hour, and I didn't even fall off my paddle board! It was the greatest fun I have had!

Stand up paddle boarding with Tony Henry (Cockroaches) and son Theo Henry.

Stand up paddle boarding Theo Henry.

Then Theo drove us back to catch the bus back to Sydney and gave us a short tour of Avalon before he dropped us at the bus stop.

When Theo was young, he was one of the children in *The Wiggles* video called "Wiggly Big Show," released in 1999. Theo now had his own band called *Apollo Hooks.* They were playing the next Saturday in Sydney, but unfortunately, we already had tickets to see *The Wiggles* that day and weren't able to go see his band. *Apollo Hooks* has since disbanded, and he is now playing in another band called *Marvell.* I hope when I go back to Australia again I can go back to Tony's place and also to see Theo's band.

On December 11th, we took the train up to Wollongong, which is 42 miles south of downtown Sydney, to see *The Wiggles.* We stayed at the Best Western City Sand hotel. It was very centrally located just a block or two from the train station and less than a half mile from the *WIN Entertainment Center* where *The Wiggles* had their show. It was also only a couple blocks from the beach.

Yahya at Win Entertainment Centre.

We went to the *WIN Entertainment Center* on December 12th and found our seats. We looked around the venue and saw Paul Field near the sound board. I walked up to him and introduced myself and told him we came from Phoenix to see the show. He was so surprised to see me. He introduced me to another crew member, Kimberly. We chatted for a while, and she arranged for us to go backstage to meet with the guys after the first show. We then enjoyed the "Wiggles Big Show" tour and everyone had a great time.

The second half of the show was a new show called "Cinder Emma." It told the story of Cinder Emma and Prince Curly Locks falling in love. Anthony was the narrator/fairy godfather, Lachy was Prince Curly Locks, Emma was Cinder Emma, and finally Simon and Captain Feathersword were the naughty sisters. It was very funny, and I had an awesome time. I wish they had included Cinder Emma in their US shows but you can find it on *YouTube.*

After the show, Kimberly took us backstage, and we met with the Wiggles. Even though they were used to seeing me in different places, they were totally shocked that I came to Australia!

Yahya with Wiggles.

Yahya with Paul Field.

Yahya with Lachy and Simon.

Yahya with Anthony and Simon.

Anthony asked what we were doing there, and I said, "Well you haven't been to Phoenix in a while, so we had to come here." Again, we brought some gifts. I made an engagement card for Emma and Lachy. My friend Andy who is also autistic, has a sewing business. He had a beautiful "Our Lady of Guadalupe" throw pillow which we bought and gave to Anthony as I knew he was Catholic.

I told him that it was made by my friend who was also autistic, and he couldn't believe it because it was so beautiful and the workmanship was perfect. Anthony mentioned to us that Greg would be doing a *Butterscotch's Playground* show in North Ryde the next day.

We stayed to watch the afternoon show and then went back to the hotel to pack and return to Sydney. The next morning, December 13th, we took the train to North Ryde which is about 8 miles from Sydney and settled in at the Courtyard by Marriott. Then we went to get tickets for Greg's show. I was broken-hearted when we were told it was sold out. My mom talked to the ticket office at the *Ryde Eastwood League Club*, explaining that we just found out about the show, and we came all the way from the US, and we were friends with Greg. After a brief hold, someone came back onto the line and said we could come to the concert, and they would set up two more chairs for us. I was ecstatic. I was going to see Greg again!

We went early because we didn't know the venue or how the seating worked. We found some seats near the stage and decided to sit and wait. A while later, Greg walked out onto the stage to set up and do sound checks. He looked out at us and just stopped and stared. Then he gave us a huge smile and said when he was finished with setting up, he would come out and talk to us.

Yahya with Greg at Butterscotch.

He came to the table we were sitting at and asked me all kinds of questions – how I was, how I found out about the show, what was I doing while I was in Australia, and what was I doing in Australia? He thought it was great that I was able to visit. He looked very healthy again and said he was feeling much better. He sat with me and my mom chatting about anything and everything and then it was time for him to go backstage and get ready for the show.

Yahya and Greg.

Anthony had told us he and Emma and Lachy would also be attending Greg's show. I saw Anthony and Emma arrive and chatted with them for a few minutes. Anthony said Lachy was not able to attend the show so they had invited Caterina to go with them.

Butterscotch's Playground was great. There was a lot of singing and dancing and fun. After the show, Greg came out and invited us backstage to chat some more. He even offered us a ride back to our hotel if we didn't mind waiting until he was all packed up. I told him how much I loved this new show of his and asked if he felt okay after all that dancing around. He said he did, that as long as he didn't overdo things, he could do one show.

The next day, we met with another *Wiggles Message Board* friend, Rachel, for lunch. She was about my age and had been a big Wiggles fan all her life and said she liked Greg the best. We all chatted, and she said she was into *Dr. Who* now. She brought a lovely *Dr. Who* program book to give to us. It was a lot of fun meeting her.

On December 15th, we took a train to Newcastle which is about an hour and 45-minute ride. We settled in our hotel, Quality Inn and took a walk on the beach. The next day I went to *The Wiggles* concert at *Newcastle Entertainment Centre.* Kimberly had arranged another meet and greet with the Wiggles before the first show. They did regular meet and greets with special needs children just like they did in the US. There were a few families there and we all got a few minutes of chit-chat and a picture.

Yahya with Wiggles and Captain Feathersword

Yahya with The Wiggles.

Then we waited for the morning show to start. It was great (the same show I saw in Wollongong but still great)! I talked again with Kimberly and told her how nice it had been meeting her and how much I appreciated her arranging the meetings with the Wiggles and said good-bye.

I was hoping to see Murray with his band, *Bang Shang A Lang* but I found out that they had disbanded the previous year.

After four *Wiggles* shows, one Greg Page show, and much sightseeing, it was time to come back home. I saw so much that I would never have imaged seeing. I held a koala. I loved riding the trains – Sydney has a great public transportation system. I met people who were only names to me before and I had more fun than I had ever had in my life! I felt sad that we were leaving but knew that I would come to Australia again someday.

Wiggly Weddings

In May 2015, Lachy and Emma got engaged. What fun – there was going to be a Wiggly wedding! They married in Bowral on April 9, 2016. It was a fairytale wedding with 200 guests.

In early 2016, there was more great Wiggly news! Simon and his girlfriend Lauren Hannaford got engaged. Lauren was once with the Wiggles playing Dorothy the Dinosaur as well as Wags the Dog and Henry the Octopus back in 2010. They were married on January 15, 2017.

The new Wiggles were fitting in well into the Wiggly world.

In February 2016, the Wiggles held a reunion concert for the over-18 crowd. All of their fans who knew and loved them as children were now adults with children of their own. Anthony and his mates Greg, Jeff, and Murray got together and performed at the *Dee Why RSL* in Sydney on February 26th with all proceeds going to the charity "Soldier On." It was such a smashing success that they performed together again on September 9th at the *Croxton Bandroom* in Melbourne and on December 16th at the *Revesby Workers Club* for the "Soldier On" charity and the over-18 fans.

When we got back from Australia, I signed up for some dance classes at Chandler/Gilbert Community College. I took a variety of types of dancing and performed in the school's dance shows. In 2017, in addition to the dance courses, I began taking courses for a multimedia certificate. I took classes such as Photoshop, Video Editing, and Animation. Animation was extremely hard, so I concentrated on the Video Editing which I loved. I took all the Video Editing classes the school offered even if they weren't required for my certificate. In 2019, I finished my classes for multimedia and now have finished with my schooling, although I still take dance lessons at Paragon Dance Studio every Friday for social dancing and occasionally on Monday.

In 2017, Greg Page created another great show. It was called "Two by 2." It had a religious theme but with a lot of good moral lessons on how to be a good person and to help others. Nowadays you can watch it on *YouTube.* It was a great show and I'm sorry it didn't catch on here.

Murray Cook joined a new band in 2017, the *Soul Movers* with Lizzie Mack. Their first album was released on September 27, 2017, "Testify." In 2019, they traveled to the US to record their third album, "Bona Fide." I like this one the best.

Spreckels Theater

On June 3, 2018, *The Wiggles* were at the *Spreckels Theater* in San Diego. To change things up, I brought Dorothy some beautiful wooden roses and some Scooby snacks for Wags. Paul Paddick was not with them on this tour and Anthony's nephew, Dominic Field, played the Captain. We saw him outside the venue before the show and when I introduced myself, he said "Oh, you're Yahya, I have heard a lot about you."

Yahya and Dominic Field.

I asked him if I could go backstage and talk to the rest of the guys. He checked and said he would bring me back after the show. Simon came out first and I gave him an engagement card that I made for him and Lauren. Then Anthony, Lachy, and Emma came out with a couple of the dancers, Caterina and Lucy.

Yahya and Wiggles.

Yahya with Simon (above) & Lachy (below).

I gave Emma a flash drive that had a video that I had made for her and Lachy's marriage. Since I went to school for Video Editing, I spend my time making a lot of videos, although most of them cannot be put on *YouTube* because of copyright stuff. I make them and watch them for my own enjoyment.

Before the show, we decided to walk around and look at the city. I did some window shopping at the stores and even saw a view of the ocean. As it was getting close to show time, we started back toward the theater. All of a sudden, we heard a lot of sirens stopping in the general area of the theater. As we turned the corner, I noticed that there were no people on the street. I thought maybe the doors had opened and everyone was already in their seat. Then I noticed the police lined up on the deserted street every few feet. A police officer came up to us and said there was an active shooter in the area and we had to get off the street.

The venue was about four buildings from where we were. My mom told me to run as fast as I could, and once in the theater, to get as far away from the street doors as I could. Well, the theater had not yet opened the doors for the fans to get to their seats (still about 20 minutes until show time) and there were probably at least 1400 people crowded into that little lobby, waiting. I felt very scared and nervous.

Everything turned out good. Everyone was safe. We only had to wait 10-15 minutes in that lobby before the doors opened. *The Wiggles* treated everyone to a fantastic show. When the show was over, the police were gone, and I saw on the news that the shooter was in a parking structure about a block from the *Spreckels Theater* and was taken into custody without anyone being hurt or any shots fired.

Making Travel Plans

On August 5, 2019, The Wiggles returned to Phoenix to perform at the *Orpheum Theater.* Since *The Wiggles* weren't doing any meet and greets on this tour, I went to the stage door and asked the guard to give them a message. He returned and said they would come and bring me backstage before the show and I should wait there. Luke Field, their current manager, arrived shortly to bring me backstage. Since the show was to start in about 15 minutes, it was a quick chat, a couple of pictures and I gave Emma a collage that I made.

Yahya with Dominic and Luke Field.

Yahya and Paul Paddick.

Yahya and Wiggles.

We then went to our seats and watched the show. This was the first time they were in Phoenix in six years. There was a good- sized crowd, everyone still remembered the Wiggles and there were a lot of younger faces of first time Wiggles fans. Lachy collected roses in our section, and I gave him a large plush, bendable rose for Dorothy and the Scooby snacks for Wags. It is fun bringing the most creative kind of roses I can think of for Dorothy each time.

We again talked to Luke Field after the show to ask what their schedule would be in 2020. My mom said we could go to Australia again in 2020. Luke gave us some dates in the spring (fall in Australia) and in July (mid-winter in Australia). I asked him what the weather was like so I could make a decision of my travel dates. I decided on March. Earlier in the year seemed to close to make travel plans, and as it happened, it was a good thing (and a bad thing) that I didn't go in January.

Heart of the Nation

Tragedy happened in Australia in January 2020. It was an extremely dry hot summer and the brushfires had gotten out of control. Australia was burning. Animals were getting sick and losing their homes with no water or food. People were losing their homes and lives. Firefighters were trying their best, but the brushfires were winning. People all over the world were helping. Stars were donating money to help. Elton John announced at one of his concerts that he was donating a million dollars to help Australia. There were billboards all over Phoenix asking for people to help Australia. I made a video to help show people what was happening over there. You can see it on *YouTube* if you search for "Australia Fires - Out of sight, Out of Mind" by Phoenix Yahya.

The original *Wiggles* (now known as the *OG Wiggles*) also wanted to help. They had a reunion show with all the proceeds going to the Australia Red Cross to help in the efforts to contain the brushfires. Two shows were held at the *Castle Hill RSL* on January 17th and January 18th, 2020, as well as live streaming the shows with pay-per-view. It was a star-spangled line-up. Opening the show was Nathan Foley from *Hi-5*. Then the *Soul Movers* with Murray Cook and Lizzie Mack, and finally the original Wiggles, Anthony Field, Greg Page, Jeff Fatt, and Murray Cook joining them after his show with the *Soul Movers*.

The evening was a huge success! The place was rockin'. Everyone was having a blast. Then more tragedy in Australia. At the end of the Wiggles set, as they were finishing "Get Ready To Wiggle," and were walking off the stage, Greg collapsed onto the stage. He had suffered a sudden cardiac arrest which means the heart cannot pump blood to the rest of the body including the brain and lungs. Thanks to the immediate response of the crew who started giving him CPR as he was not breathing and did not have a pulse, and the quick thinking of another person getting the AED (automated external defibrillator), and shocking him with it three times, Greg survived. His heart was beating when the ambulance arrived 20 minutes later.

Statistics show that each year, approximately 30,000 people suffer from sudden cardiac arrest within Australia. Most of these occur outside of the hospital. The survival rate for someone who has a cardiac arrest outside of the hospital is only 10%. That means that for every one person that survives the cardiac arrest outside of a hospital, nine people die. Can you imagine? That is one of the scariest survival rates in the world.

You can help though. By knowing CPR and performing CPR, along with early defibrillator use, you can increase the chance of survival by around 70%. The statistics say that for every minute without a defibrillator, the chance of survival decreases by approximately 10%. If they hadn't started life-saving measures on Greg, he would have had zero to minimal chances of survival, having had to wait approximately 20 minutes for the ambulance.

Since Greg was in the hospital, the second "Brushfire Relief" show paid tribute to him with six yellow Wiggles on stage. Paul and John Field, Jack Gatto, Paul Paddick, Simon Pryce, and Emma Watkins. Although everyone was sad, it turned out to be an awesome show.

When Greg was released from the hospital, he felt so thankful to be alive that he made it his mission to educate people about the importance of knowing CPR, and about public and private buildings have AEDs readily available in case of emergencies. Greg now runs *Heart of the Nation.* It is a non-profit organization whose goal is to get as many AEDs into the community as possible. This is not an easy task. This has become his main focus and passion.

Greg Page and *Heart of the Nation* had a live streaming CPR training class and Greg wanted to set a record for the largest number of people involved in a CPR and AED training class. As he personally knows, any attempt at resuscitation is better than no attempt and he wants everyone to have the knowledge and the confidence to be able to perform CPR if they ever need to. October 16th is "World Restart the Heart Day." This live streaming class was held on October 16th at 3:00 p.m. Joining Greg on this record-setting day was Daniel Gay from *Surf Life Saving Australia*, who taught the CPR class, showing the viewers easy-to-learn techniques for adults and children. There were also demonstrations with cricket legend Brett Lee, Mitch and Mark from *The Block* and other special guests who showed just how easy it is for anyone to learn this simple chain of survival (Call emergency responders, push the chest and shock with the AED). This event has had over 25,000 views.

Greg has even written a song so that everyone, even young children, will understand and know what to do should the need arise. The song is "Keep the Beat Going." It is a fun way of remembering the steps to CPR – first check for safety, check the victim, call for help and finally do compression on the chest until they are breathing. You can find both the virtual CPR class and Greg's song on *YouTube*.

My second trip to Australia was quickly approaching. I had tickets to see 4-5 Wiggles shows. The *Sacred Hearts* (consisting of Jeff Fatt, Tony Henry and Paul Field) were playing at the *Canterbury League Club* in Belmore which is a suburb of Sydney. John Field was also playing there while we were in Australia, and the *Soul Movers* have several gigs scheduled near Sydney while we would be there. I knew this trip is going to be bigger and better than my last trip. We were scheduled to leave on March 18, 2020, and return on April 15, 2020. I was so excited. I was already packed and had some artisan wooden roses for Dorothy. I did buy some Scooby snacks but didn't know whether they would survive the trip or get crunched into tiny pieces.

Then tragedy strikes again, as the world is rocked with news of a deadly virus, called the

Coronavirus. Events were being cancelled and places were closing to avoid the spread of the Coronavirus. On March 16th, two days before we were to leave, the majority of Australia hadn't cancelled anything yet and I still wanted to continue my plans. My mom was nervous but agreed with me about not cancelling. On March 18th, the day of our flight, I heard that *The Wiggles* had postponed all their March and April concerts due to the Coronavirus. Since that was the main part of our trip, we decided to postpone the trip. Then the following day, March 19th, we heard that *Canterbury League Club* had cancelled all the concerts scheduled and I figured it was probably for the best that we didn't go to Australia. We would reschedule our trip when this virus had been contained.

The whole world was in a lockdown due to the Covid-19 pandemic. The worst was yet to come. It seemed to peak in April and the number of cases started going down. Then again in the winter, the number of cases started rising again. Nothing seemed to be able to help keep this pandemic under control.

All shows and live performances were cancelled indefinitely.

In May 2020, *The Wiggles* decided if they couldn't play live to their audiences, they would perform a virtual concert in their *Hot Potato Studio* on *Facebook Live.* You can still see it on *YouTube* and it has almost 34,000 views.

They also played a virtual concert at the *Sydney Opera House* on June 14, 2020. You can also see this concert on *YouTube.*

By the end of June, the world was getting cabin fever from being under lockdown, so the *OG Wiggles* (formerly known as the original *Wiggles*) had teamed up with their mate Murray Cook and the *Soul Movers* to film a special music video called "Circles Baby," an exercise video that would get everyone up and dancing, get their hearts pumping and get everyone having fun again. This was released on July 22nd and you can see it on *YouTube.*

The Coronavirus was showing some signs of abating by the end of 2020 and some of the restrictions were lifted. *The Wiggles* performed a special one-time concert at the *Sydney Coliseum Theater* on December 19, 2020, called "Wiggly Christmas Big Show." There were all kinds of special precautions in place for this show. Fans had to get their temperature taken upon entering the venue. Hand sanitizing stations were placed throughout the venue, and seating would be in accordance with the social distancing policy. Any items that the fans brought for the Wiggles or their friends, like roses, were to be put in a basket so that *The Wiggles* could collect them after the show.

Wiggle Around Covid

Finally, a vaccine was developed. Not everyone was taking it, but I got mine on January 19th and February 16th of 2021. Now hopefully the world would settle back to normal and countries would again open their borders to visitors.

Some sad news comes from the Wiggles' world during this pandemic. Emma announced that she is retiring as the yellow Wiggle after more than a decade of performing with *The Wiggles.* She will return to studying at the university to get her Ph.D. and continuing to work with the deaf community, a place that is very dear to her heart. I can't believe that she has been with them for that long. It seems like only a few years. Time passes so quickly.

A new yellow Wiggle was chosen to replace Emma. She is 16-year-old Tsehay Hawkins who is brand new to *The Wiggles* organization. She was chosen to play the red Wiggle in *Fruit Salad TV* and after only two episodes, she got word that she was chosen to be the new yellow Wiggle. She is the youngest Wiggle, the second female Australian Wiggle, and the first Wiggle of color (she is Ethiopian-Australia). Good luck to you Tsehay. I can't wait to meet you in person!

Coincidentally on the same day that Emma announced she was leaving, there was some exciting and happy news from the Wiggles' world. *The Wiggles* announced that the OG Wiggles were reuniting and going on tour throughout Australia in 2022. This is the third time since their retirement that *The Wiggles* have gotten together for an over-21 show. This time, they will be doing seven shows from February through May 2022. They will basically be following the same schedule as the new Wiggles concert tour in 2022, playing pretty much the same venues, only the shows will start at 8:00 p.m. and only fans over 18 will be allowed in.

In the news from Australia, they are tentatively planning to open their borders for travel into and out of the country in the near future, and *The Wiggles* are planning a North American tour in 2022. It sounds like the world is recovering from Covid-19 and things will be getting back to normal soon and I can start my next two decades with *The Wiggles.* Hopefully I can start planning by next trip to Australia soon. I also wish the *OG Wiggles* would bring their show to the US. It would be great to see the guys together again and I know that they have many Wiggles fans here in the US who wish the same thing.

I have my treasured memories with *The Wiggles* from the past 30 years and now it's time for a new chapter in my life with the new *Wiggles.* But the question is "Why are there eight Wiggles now in their new lineup" and "Will I like the new yellow Wiggle since Emma is no longer in *The Wiggles.*" We'll see, I guess I will find out. Who knows? I just know that I love being friends with *The Wiggles* and seeing them when I can.

Yahya's Next Great Adventure

Now that I know where *The Wiggles* come from, and I have treasured memories with them for the past 30 years, I thought that writing this book was the perfect way to celebrate *The Wiggles* 30th birthday and our friendship of nearly as long.

I have traveled to many places to see them, like the United Kingdom and Australia, and many different cities in the United States. I have met a lot of wonderful people who also love *The Wiggles.*

I have also traveled to a lot of exotic places like Sweden, Istanbul, Egypt, and even Canada, for vacations, not to see *The Wiggles.* I took a cruise to Mexico for my 25th birthday. It was a Halloween cruise and I dressed up as Harry Potter. I won a Harry Potter trivia contest on board, getting extra points for my authentic costume including having the scar (made with makeup). There were also dance classes aboard which I participated in.

Dance class on cruise to Mexico 2018.

When I was 12, in 2006, I met Br. Dawud Wharnsby in California. He was such a wonderful person. Soon after we met, he sent me a CD that he personally recorded of his favorite songs. He still keeps in touch with me by email and I have been able to see him several times since then.

I still love listening to music, making videos, watching movies, dancing and especially traveling.

My thoughts about the future are to be able to live in my own place, continue writing and making videos and to have the opportunity to travel. There are so many places in the world that I want to see.

About The Author

Yahya Lutfi, from Tempe, Arizona, describes himself as a friendly and helpful guy. He's been working since he was 18 years old, and he's worked at places like the Marriott Hotel, Bath and Body Works, and even a tortilla factory!

Aside from being a Wiggles superfan, some of his other interests include dancing, video editing, and watching movies like Harry Potter and his current favorite TV show, Cobra Kai.

He enjoys traveling, and some of his adventures have taken him to Australia (where the Wiggles are from), London, Sweden, Istanbul, and Canada. For his 25th birthday, he went on a Mexican cruise, which was one of his favorite trips.

Yahya's long-term goal is to live independently and to continue writing, making videos, and traveling.

Yahya believes that people with Autism Spectrum Disorder can achieve anything.

Mom's Afterword

Yahya was diagnosed with Autism when he was 20 months old, right after we moved to Arizona. He was started in early intervention soon after that, which was really amazing considering there is usually quite a long waiting list for services.

He never really had a lot of words before he was diagnosed, but right around his second birthday, he pretty much became non-verbal. He had a lot of ear infections, sometimes even 2-3 a month and I kept asking doctors if it was possible that he wasn't hearing clearly or if the ear infections were somehow a factor in his not speaking. They just told me that I was in denial, and he was not speaking because he was autistic.

Finally, one of his doctors agreed to put tubes in his ears when he was three years old and from that point, he started talking little by little, first single words and then progressing from there. So yes, he was autistic, but the fact that he didn't speak apparently had more to do with his hearing than his autism.

We tried a lot of different ways to teach Yahya and the best way seemed to be by video. There were many different types of teaching videos for children with special needs and I think we tried them all. Not a lot of things, even videos, caught Yahya's attention.

In 1996, I heard of some videos called "*Special Kids*" made by a couple just outside of Milwaukee who had an autistic son and they found that these videos worked well for their son. I ordered one, but didn't think it would work as there wasn't any music or dancing in it. It was just the father on screen repeating the word and generalizing it in different ways, by showing a picture, showing the object, and spelling the word.

When I put it in the video player, Yahya was fascinated. I had been trying to teach him colors and shapes for several weeks, but when he watched the *Special Kids* video, he learned his colors and shapes in one day. I ended up ordering the whole set it worked so well.

Yahya also watched Captain Kangaroo when he was young. In 1997, there was segment that the Captain said "*It's Wiggle Time*" and four guys in solid-colored shirts sang a song and danced. Yahya was fascinated. They sang a song called "*Fruit Salad.*" All about the wonders of eating healthy foods like a combination of different fruits in one bowl.

Yahya had always been a picky eater. Besides having a very limited diet, everything he ate had to be on a separate plate, no foods could come in contact with other foods. If he ordered a burger and fries, the burger had to be on one plate, the fries on another plate and if it came with a pickle or anything, that had to be on another plate. Or if he wanted fruit, each kind of fruit had to be on a different plate.

When he heard the song "*Fruit Salad*" and decided to see what it would be like if he put all of his food together like that. Wow, amazing! It was not a bad thing to have food mixed together. It was quite good.

After that, he was able to enjoy his burger and fries on the same plate. He mixed his lentil soup with his falafel and some vegetables. Thanks to the Wiggles, he no longer is a picky eater and he no longer has to have separate plates for each food.

In 2002, *The Wiggles* came to Phoenix. Yahya was so excited when he found out we were going. When Murray went into the audience to collect roses, we didn't know about this tradition so we didn't have any, but I had a business card that I had written a short note about Yahya being autistic and asking if he could meet them after the show. I handed it to him as he passed, and he stopped to watch as I prompted Yahya to keep doing the movements that the people on stage were doing.

Murray asked a couple of questions about him and told me that he would talk to the other guys and see if they could arrange a short meeting. Then he continued on to collect roses.

With any other "celebrity," I would have wondered about that answer. However, as soon as Murray got back on stage, he went up to each of the other Wiggles and talked and pointed to us and talked some more. Then a security person came up to us and asked us to wait in our seat after the show and we would be taken back stage. I was very impressed with these guys!

When we got back stage, Paul, Murray, Jeff and Greg were sitting at a table and Yahya sat at the table with them. I stood back and watched (and took a couple of pictures). I felt kind of bad that they tried so hard to interact with Yahya and he didn't respond. I wanted to go up to the table and help out, but I wanted Yahya to do this on his own. Once Jeff finally got him to answer a question, Yahya just kept on talking and answering them like they were old friends.

Sticker reward charts were a big part of his therapy. We would set the reward (something like getting an ice cream or eating at McDonalds) and then tell him how many stickers it will take to get it. I was always pretty generous with stickers so he could earn the reward in a day or two. When I saw how much he loved *The Wiggles* show and found out that they would be in Minneapolis and Madison in a couple of months, I suggested a sticker chart for going to see *The Wiggles* again. I told him he had to earn 200 stickers in two months. That was one of the best summers I have had because he was trying so hard to be good and earn his stickers. In fact, he earned way more than 200 stickers at the end of the two months. He was very happy to see *The Wiggles* again in both cities and even more so because they remembered him. I was amazed that they remembered him from one meeting in a totally different city more than two months earlier. These are very special guys.

I sent a few of the pictures that I took of Yahya meeting the Wiggles at these shows to them in Australia. There was one picture of Yahya and Greg and you could just see Yahya glowing with happiness. A while later, I received an envelope from Australia. Paul Field, their manager, had written back to me thanking me for the lovely pictures and enclosing an autographed pictures of the Wiggles and friends.

Then, one of my friends from the Wiggles Message Board asked me if that was a picture of Yahya in the latest issue of *The Wiggles Magazine.* I didn't know what she was talking about since I didn't subscribe to the magazine. She sent me the picture and sure enough, it was the picture I had sent of Yahya and Greg. It was a total surprise because no one had told me they were going to be doing that. It made Yahya really happy though.

At the time, I had a website that sold the new line of Wiggles toys in the US, and I had also put that picture on my website. I received an email from someone associated with *The Wiggles* requesting that I take that picture off my website as it belonged to *The Wiggles.* That confused me as it was my picture and I got such a nice letter from Paul, so I replied that it was my picture that I had taken after a show, and I had sent it to *The Wiggles* to show them how happy they made my son. It was apparently some kind of misunderstanding as I never heard from that person again.

For the next few years, *The Wiggles* stopped in Phoenix when they toured the US. Although we went to see them each time, sometimes for one show and sometimes for all the shows, I didn't ask for a meet-and-greet each time. With autism, things become a routine and I didn't want his seeing *The Wiggles* to become a routine – go to Wiggles concert, meet the Wiggles and say hi and then go home. It would mean more if it was spontaneous, so I was very glad that the years that Yahya didn't do a meet-and-greet, they acknowledged him in other ways. That made seeing them special each time.

Although language has always been difficult for Yahya, he has always been fascinated by other languages. Every time he watched anything on video, he put the subtitles to another language, or he put the speaking to another language and the subtitles to English. So, he was really excited when he saw *The Taiwanese Wiggles.* He loved watching them sing familiar Wiggles songs but in another language. *The Spanish Wiggles* were even more exciting because he had taken a year of Spanish in eighth grade and knew a bit of Spanish.

I always tried to get Yahya involved in any activity that he showed an interest in. He liked doing Special Olympics swimming and other Special Olympics events. He usually wanted to try everything. There was also a group of his friends who got together every Saturday morning to bowl. That was something else he looked forward to.

Another thing I tried, when Yahya was 11 years old in 2005, was letting him take classes at *Childsplay*, which is a children's theater group here in Phoenix. This was the first group that he was in that was not especially for special needs children. He was the only special needs child in the group. Classes were once a week, for a month, for half a day. Yahya has a very short attention span unless it is something that he likes, then he can watch or do it for hours at a time.

In the first class, they worked on the song, *"I Just Can't Wait To Be King,"* from *The Lion King* and at the end of the classes, they performed it for the parents. He learned the song and the dance and was very well behaved in class. The teachers all said it was great having him in class.

From there, I let him go to *Ahwatukee Children's Theater*, another children's theater group where they put on entire plays and had a lot more rehearsal. His first play was *Grease* and he was in the chorus.

The director was worried about having him in the play with all typical children, but after a few days, was very pleased with him following directions and working with the other children. He continued doing plays and classes with both groups for the next couple of years.

In high school, Yahya was in regular classes with some special ed classes mixed in. He took dance all throughout high school and each year was in the dance show that the school put on. He chose a song and did the choreography for his solo dance. One year, he did a tap dance to "If You Should See Her" by the Field Brothers. He was also on the swimming team for the last two years of high school. Again, he was the only special needs swimmer on the team and the coach was very pleased with him.

I started taking Yahya to see musicals at *Gammage Auditorium* and he loved them. After high school, we went to see "Motown the Musical." Our seats were in the third or fourth row. When they were spotlighting Diana Ross, she came to the edge of the stage and asked if any of the gentlemen in the audience wanted to come up on stage and sing with her, all of the guys kind of ducked down in their seat and tried not to draw attention to themselves. Yahya asked me if he could raise his hand. He was the only one who did, and she told him to come up to on the stage. They sang "Lean on Me." Even though he didn't know the song, he did a really good job of faking it. Then he was all smiles as he came back to his seat.

Yahya has come a long way since he first met *The Wiggles* and was "star-struck" and didn't talk to them. I feel that the Wiggles were a big part of giving him the confidence to try any new thing that comes his way, and we will always be glad for their friendship.

- *Sue Lutfi*

Made in the USA
Las Vegas, NV
31 January 2022